EVEN ME, GOD?
"YES, EVEN YOU!"

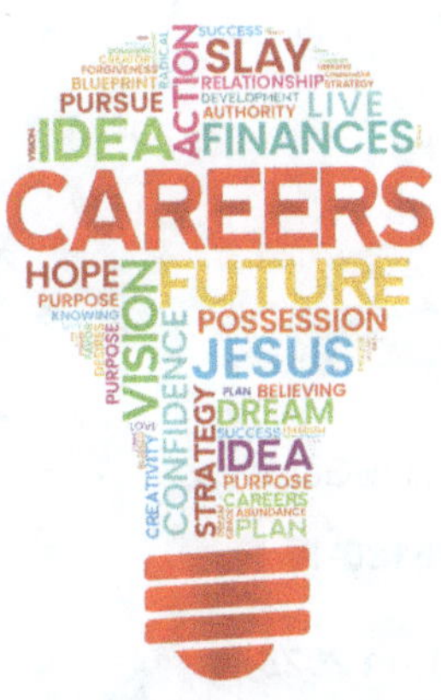

Nakita G Gates

Copyright 2023

Published by Nakita G Gates

ISBN: 979-8-218-26180-1

First printing edition 2023

Nakita G Gates

Yes@EvenMeGod.com

United States

Printed and Distributed by Ingramspark

TABLE OF CONTENTS

PREFACE

I am an Encourager. The gift God gave me is the ability to encourage; to encourage people to dream and to have hope and to know that with God, all things are possible.

This book is written for those who have an ear to hear. If you receive these words, that means it's your time to rise up and walk in your calling and to pursue the desires of your heart! You ask, "Even me, God?" God says, "Yes, even YOU!"

In the book of Jeremiah, Jeremiah the prophet was tasked by God to deliver a message that God's people would have to live, build houses, marry, pray for peace, and prosper in a city that was not theirs. Thus, the words in Jeremiah 29:11 were written:

"For I know the plans I have for you," says the Lord, "They are plans to prosper you and to not harm you, plans to give you a future and a hope."

"The ability of children to dream is a natural instinct instilled by the Creator."
- Myles Munroe

1

MY DREAM, EVEN AS A YOUNG CHILD

"Above all else, guard your heart for it affects everything you do."
Proverbs 4:23

"Take delight in the Lord and He will give you the desires of your heart." Psalms 37:4

"For I know the plans I have for you, says the Lord, plans for welfare (health-happiness-fortunes) and not for evil, to give you a future and a hope."
Jeremiah 29:11

"I have given you authority to trample on snakes and scorpions and to overcome all the power of the enemy; nothing will harm you."
Luke 10:19

"If one moves confidently in the direction of their dreams, and endeavors to live the life which he has imagined, he will meet with a success unexpected in common hours."
Henry David Thoreau

This has been a dream of mine since I was a child. I always felt like I would be encouraging others. I saw myself standing in front of a podium, speaking and crying, while my audience was crying too.

As an adult in my 20s, I had a tremendous fear of speaking and would rather die than get up and speak in front of a crowd. I never wanted the attention on me; what's great about me? Well, 20 years later, the opportunity came for me to speak at a transitional living facility, to share the story that I am sharing with you, on how to move past your fears – regardless of your circumstances – and pursue the desires of your heart.

What Were Your Dreams/Visions as a Child?

____
____
____
____
____
____
____
____
____
____
____
____
____
____
____
____

I put off the invitation for a few months because I was so scared to speak. But then I asked myself, if not now, when? I knew I had to do it because it was what I had asked God for – a purpose in life – and He gave me my ministry to go back and do for others what He had done for me. He gave me hope and a future. I asked Him for a purpose, and He gave it to me in a flash. Now in 2023, I can remember crying to the Lord, I want to do more, help more people, and He called me to write this book.

So, I accepted the invitation to speak at the transitional living facility. I was very well prepared with my notes and handouts, the same things I am sharing with you now. I stood in front of the class, pacing back and forth to calm my nerves, holding my notes tightly just in case I needed support. After introducing myself and telling them why I was there, I told them that I had a deep fear of speaking in public. But they all said there is no way they would have known that – "You don't look like you're scared." My spirit reminded me that when you are doing something for God, He will give you the strength you need to do what He has called you to do.

Many weeks before my presentation, I prayed, "Lord, I feel so empty. I don't feel like I have anything to share." But as I humbled myself before my class and God, we were all crying by the end. We were all in awe of God and how He spoke to all of us at our need, and we were so grateful for His faithfulness. He just poured through me and into them. What a blessing.

The result: When I drove to the campus in the following weeks to do my next presentations, I would see my students on the bus, dressed, ready to go… pursuing the desires of their heart. They were tired of sitting back and watching the world pass them by while everyone else was busy with life. They had my handouts held tightly, along with the scriptures. We mapped out how they would get from where they were to where they wanted to be, and we focused. Only God could do this!

The Universe must make room for you. The Universe has to make room for the manifestation of your dreams and for your calling on this earth.

"Use your imagination to communicate
and articulate your deepest desires. Once
imagination and speaking it are both
aligned, possibility explodes into existence,
and the Universe collaborates with us
to breathe life into our visions. As we
move forward confidently, the bridge of
incidents manifest, leading us to our divine
destination and many times much more."

I pray you receive this message of
encouragement and that you receive it in God's
love and His timing for the calling in your life.

Our Deepest Fear

"Our deepest fear is NOT that we are inadequate. Our deepest fear is that we are powerful beyond measure. It is our light, not our darkness, that most frightens us. We ask ourselves, who am I to be brilliant, handsome, talented, and powerful? Actually, who are you not to be? You are a child of God. Your playing small doesn't serve the world. There's nothing enlightened by shrinking so that other people won't feel insecure around

How Do You Feel After Reading This? What are your thoughts about this as it relates to you? Do you have fears limiting your potential? Please share.

____
____
____
____
____
____
____
____
____
____
____
____
____
____
____

you. We were born to make manifest the glory of God that is within us. It's not just in some of us, it's in everyone. And, as we let our own light shine, we unconsciously give others permission to do the same. As we are liberated from our own fear, our presence automatically liberates others."

- Nelson Mandela

2

YOU ARE MEANT TO LIVE AND NOT JUST TO EXIST, TO EXPERIENCE A GOOD LIFE, AND TO MAKE A DIFFERENCE!

"Above all else, guard your heart for it affects everything you do."
Proverbs 4:23

"Take delight in the Lord and He will give you the desires of your heart." Psalms 37:4

"For I know the plans I have for you, says the Lord, plans for welfare (health-happiness-fortunes) and not for evil, to give you a future and a hope."
Jeremiah 29:11

"I have given you authority to trample on snakes and scorpions and to overcome all the power of the enemy; nothing will harm you."
Luke 10:19

"If one moves confidently in the direction of their dreams, and endeavors to live the life which he has imagined, he will meet with a success unexpected in common hours."
Henry David Thoreau

Then God said, "Let us make mankind in
our image, in our likeness, so that they
may rule over the fish in the sea and the
birds in the sky, over the livestock and all
the wild animals, and over all the creatures
that move along the ground."
- Genesis 1:26

This book shares my misery in life 25 years ago when I had no hope, no purpose, no vision. I was fearful of everything and everyone. I felt like I walked around in life stooped over, asking people to forgive me for even existing. When I was a young child, my mother would always tell me and my brother that we would never be anything and that no one would love us but her. Sadly, as I grew older, I realized that was what her adopted mother told her as a child. And those words from our mother were just all we had to go on. But I always felt in my spirit that I was supposed to have more in life, experience more in life. It wasn't until I was 37 and started going to church that I learned who God really is. That He loved me, that He had a plan and purpose for ME, and that I had dominion over the earth rather than the earth having dominion over me. It was then that I listened, paid attention, and began spending time with God and the Word. I was interested. I was ready! God called me in out of the dusty world at 37 years old. Hallelujah!

God then turned my misery into a ministry to encourage people to dream and to have hope and to know that with God, all things are possible. Coming from a life with no purpose, work that I felt did not challenge my potential, God gave me purpose and the career of my desires. And please know that God will use all that you have gone through. As He promises:

> "He will bring everything to work together for the good of those who love God and are called according to His purpose for them."
>
> **- Romans 8:28**

In other words, He takes you through the valley so that you will have a testimony of how He saved you, delivered you, set you free. How else would He get us to share the good news, His Good News, of who He is, and who and whose you are?

I used to ask friends and associates, "Excuse me, what do you think I should be doing in life?" Isn't that the craziest question to ask anyone other than your Creator? People have no clue, as many aren't even sure what they are supposed to be doing in life. But they looked good. Looked like they had it all together. But God said:

"I will instruct you and teach you in the way
you should go. I will counsel you, advise
you, and watch over you with My loving
eye upon you."
- Psalm 32:8

I needed to hear that; I needed to know that. I keep this scripture very near to my heart and God has never failed me after consulting with Him. What I heard, "I spoke you here, I can very well take care of you here. Don't go to man for wise counsel, come to Me!"

So, God orchestrated me into going to a particular church. One day, my little cousins moved to Texas and said, "Cousin, cousin, we want to go to church." I wasn't going to church, but I heard of a good church to go to so off we went. We were a tad tardy, so we had to sit in overflow, which was next to the choir and pulpit. The pastor took a special interest in the children. Crazily enough, he asked that they all stand up and give their names and ages (I had three), and he thought how wonderful that they were all in church today. And that was God drawing my attention!

So, we all started going to that church every Sunday, and Bible Study on Wednesday too. I had no idea what was going on; people were crying to the Lord, "Lord, I sure do love you." The pastor was talking about Pharoh, and I'm looking around thinking, who is Pharoh? That's how clueless I was. So, I listened, engaged, intrigued by what I was hearing, and I kept attending. One day, I heard the pastor say, "God gave us dominion over the earth; the earth does not have dominion over us. We can put the devil under our feet – we have the authority, and we can stomp him once he is under our feet." I did a whole lot of stomping once I heard that.

> "I have given you authority to trample on snakes and scorpions and to overcome all the power of the enemy; nothing will harm you."
> **- Luke 10:19-20**

Wow! How excited I was to know that I had some authority – I had the big-head boxing that devil out of my life. Then God showed me the next scripture which says:

> "[20]However, do not rejoice that the spirits submit to you, but rejoice that your names are written in heaven."

So I said, "Okay, Lord."

I heard the people say, "God loves you," and the more I listened, the more I was elated to know that someone does love me. Then I could feel His arms wrap around me and hug me, and He started teaching me exactly what His love meant. I tell you, whenever I would go to church, I would cry rivers of tears; God cleansing me of all the pain I had gone through in those 37 years before He called me in.

I must tell you, as God was shedding the worldly life off me, I asked, "Lord, why do people say they love you? Please don't strike me down for asking." Well, not long afterwards, I remember crying out to God, "I sure do love You," I could hear Him say, "Now you know, now you know why people say they love Me." I was telling Him, "I sure do love You," and "Thank you," for taking me out of the dusty world, thanking Him for giving me hope and a future, my desire, and a ministry on top of that! I was saying, "Lord, I love you," for loving me, delivering me, and setting me free- free from bondage it felt like! I tell you, there is no better love than God's, and once you receive that love, you won't go looking for love in all the wrong places. His assured love will keep you out of a lot of trouble. He created us to desire Him! It was me, I was the one who asked God, "Even ME God," and He said, "Yes, even YOU, Nakita!"

The business (my desire) and the ministry (my misery in the world), God gave me. One day, I sat in my living room writing out my business plan and ministry, and after reading it, I said, this is from God because I am not even smart enough to have come up with something this good. It was amazing. Twenty years later, I am still amazed at the words

He gave me to write. He will do it!

My book takes you through all the steps and scriptures God gave me on how to pursue the desires of my heart. How to walk without fear, how to have confidence in God, dreaming, accomplishing dreams, free, liberated, hopeful, loved, and kept.

"I will bless you and keep you, I will smile upon you and show you my graciousness, I will give you My favor and My peace," says the Lord.
- Numbers 6:24-26

Know that NO MATTER where you are today in life, God wants you to succeed on this earth. We are spiritual beings having an earthly experience, don't forget that! Let go of how and just... align, believe, relax, and let it happen!

I'll see you at the pinnacle of your dreams!

3

HOW TO PURSUE THE DESIRES OF YOUR HEART FOR CAREER AND PURPOSE, REMEMBERING YOU WERE GIVEN DOMINION OVER THE EARTH, THE EARTH DOES NOT HAVE DOMINION OVER YOU ~ ENJOY!

"Above all else, guard your heart for it affects everything you do."
Proverbs 4:23

"Take delight in the Lord and He will give you the desires of your heart." Psalms 37:4

"For I know the plans I have for you, says the Lord, plans for welfare (health-happiness-fortunes) and not for evil, to give you a future and a hope."
Jeremiah 29:11

"I have given you authority to trample on snakes and scorpions and to overcome all the power of the enemy; nothing will harm you."
Luke 10:19

"If one moves confidently in the direction of their dreams, and endeavors to live the life which he has imagined, he will meet with a success unexpected in common hours."
Henry David Thoreau

Why is it important to write down your vision?

Having a written personal vision allows you to plan the most efficient course to your goals. It allows you to have the clarity of when to say "yes" or "no" to things based on your own personal values and vision. It also helps you to spot potential hazards or roadblocks before you're impacted by them.

Write your vision, make it plain.

(Don't be afraid, write it down – it may even scare you but if it is in your heart, God wants you to get there and enjoy the journey – He is going to use it all for His glory). Don't share your vision with others until your footing is sure. This is between you and God, God and you.

____

____

____

____

You ask, "Even me, God? God answers, "Yes, even you."

Keep writing... get it all on paper!

Now, lay it before the Lord and ask Him to bless it and to give you clarity and direction all the while being still and quiet. You will feel His peace but you may be shaking... because it's exciting!!! It's exciting to be in charge of your life, to do what God has put in your heart.

> Trust in the LORD with all your heart and lean not on your own understanding; in all your ways submit to him, and He will make your paths straight.
> **- Proverbs 3:5-6**

Now, we are ready to write the action plan – how to get there! Here is the fun part of living and not just existing. You have a plan; you have purpose!

The Righteous Shall Live by His Faith - And the LORD answered me: "Write the vision; make it plain on tablets, so he may run who reads it. For still the vision awaits its appointed time; it speaks of the end — it will not lie. If it seems slow, wait for it; because it will surely come and it will not delay."
- Habakkuk 2:2-3:

"If one moves confidently in the direction of their dreams, and endeavors to live the life which he has imagined, he will meet with a success unexpected in common hours."
- Henry David Thoreau

You have your vision; now what? No matter where you are today in life — regardless of your circumstances — you can STILL manifest and live your dreams, the desires of your heart! We were created as spiritual royalty, and we have a divine inheritance; you have to trust your Creator and commit to Him.

Trust in the Lord and do good; dwell
in the land and enjoy safe pasture.
Take delight in the Lᴏʀᴅ, and He will
give you the desires of your heart.
⁵ Commit your way to the Lᴏʀᴅ; trust
in Him and He will do this.
- Psalm 37:4-5

The Lord is my shepherd **(that's
Relationship!)**
I shall not want **(that's Supply!)**
He maketh me to lie down in green
pastures **(that's Rest)**
He leadeth me beside the still
waters **(that's Refreshment!)**
He restoreth my soul **(that's
Healing!)**
He leadeth me in the paths of
righteousness **(that's Guidance!)**
For His name's sake **(that's
Purpose!)**
Yea, though I walk through the
valley of the shadow of death
(that's Testing!)

I will fear no evil **(that's Protection!)**
For thou art with me **(that's Faithfulness!)**
Thy rod and thy staff they comfort me **(that's Discipline!)**
Thou preparest a table before me in the presence of mine enemies **(that's Hope!)**
Thou anointest my head with oil **(that's Consecration!)**
My cup runneth over **(that's Abundance!)**
Surely goodness and mercy shall follow me all the days of my life **(that's Blessing!)**
And I will dwell in the house of the LORD **(that's Security!)**
Forever **(that's Eternity!)**
- Psalm 23

Remember, He has a plan and purpose for us ALL. We ALL have work to do — build houses, prosper in a city that is not ours. Let's get busy!

And as you will come to know, <u>there is absolutely nothing more satisfying to your soul than to move confidently into the plans and purpose God has for you</u>.

> "And you shall seek Me, and find Me, when you search for me with all your heart."
> **- Jeremiah 29:13**

Here is your strategy to manifest your dreams and pursue the desires of your heart:

First, let me say again, do not tell everyone your dream. Not everyone is going to be your champion, and you are already possibly walking in fear; you certainly do not need any help with that! Stay focused on what God says about your strategy and keep it moving. Put blinders on your face and do not look to the left or to the right — both are distractions — but straight ahead with your plan and scriptures. I can tell you there is going to be a lot of fear, and the enemy is going to continue to ask you like he asked me, "Girl, who do you think you are – go sit down." So you reply, "Not today, devil, not today," and push him out of the way and stomp him with the Word of God. That is what I had to do until I was not trembling... as much! God's got you, believe me — BELIEVE HIM!

"Above all else, guard your heart for it affects everything you do."
- Proverbs 4:23

"Behold, I give unto you power to tread on serpents and scorpions, and over all the power of the enemy: and nothing shall by any means hurt you."
- Luke 10:19

So, you have dreams to be the/a president, a movie star, a businessperson, a missionary/nun, a journalist, an educator. Whatever dream you have in your heart but may feel so undeserving of, you now have your armor. You are ready and trusting God and committing to doing it no matter how scared you are because if God says I can have a better life in Him, than dog-gone-it, I am going for it! I want to be free. I want to be liberated. I want to help others! I want to love and be loved.

An example of your strategy: If you want to be the President — because that's how far out the dreams that God gives us are. It scares us, and we can only do it with HIM — you will map out a plan of how to get to the White House.

Instruction: Based upon where you are today, with the knowledge and skills you have, what else do you need to learn? What else do you need to do to get there? So, you map it out step by step, checking off each step as you achieve it, and going to the next step until you are in the White House. (Yeah!)

Now, beware. You will hear whispers in your head telling you that you are not good enough for any of your steps as you move through them. Remember, the enemy is enjoying you where you are – he does not want to see you moving away from your low self-esteem, being scared and not knowing who you are and what you are, so he can wreak havoc in your life. You may get some no's when you go knocking on doors while saying to yourself, "I need this step to get to the next one." But you know what? You cannot get dismayed or swayed by the no's because you know that is what you must have, so you continue to knock on the doors until you get a yes. Once you have accomplished that, you go to the next step of your strategy and continue to climb your ladder to your desire. God will open the doors.

"I have set before thee an open
door, and no man can shut it."
- **Revelation 3:8**

I have been told many times, by several people, that when God closes one door, He opens another. There can be doors of opportunities; doors that lead you from one place to another.

You will be successful in getting to that yes because people will see how passionate you are (people like passion), and that your passion is coming from you knowing... you need that YES.

"Ask, and the gift is yours. Seek, and
you'll discover. Knock, and the door will
be opened for you. For every persistent
one will get what he asks for."
- **Matthew 7:7-8**

You are focused. Push that door down – not giving up. Get your scriptures out and repeat, "God says this about me and my situation…" Get back up every day and keep pushing because guess what, if you don't push that door until it opens, it will never open. I promise you will be okay, just keep moving – don't give up! Keep praying, keep believing, and before you know it, you will be so amazed as you will be where you mapped out yourself to be. Keep your vision in front of you, continue to pray over it, thank God, revise it as needed, but keep moving and keep stomping the devil.

> "God would not have put a dream in your
> heart if He had not given you everything
> you need to fulfill it. Confidence is going
> after Moby Dick in a rowboat and taking
> the tartar sauce with you."
> **- Anonymous**

I am so excited for you! Now go, live your best life and pull someone else up while you are doing it. I am always stopping to encourage someone who looks like they forgot whose they are. God has a plan and hope for ALL of us. You should see God work! He will work through us to help others. As you liberate yourself, you are able to liberate others. God has given me the gift to speak to others in low places and in high places and be received. God put on my heart to pray for that. For what has He put on your heart to pray?

How Much More, Lord!

This morning I asked, "How much more
can I take. What else must I do for Your
name's sake?"
I'm running this race to get closer to You.
But, my God, I can't believe the things I go
through.
The stress and struggles of this thing
called life. The unknowns – will I be a good
husband or get a good wife?
What school shall I attend, Masters,
Doctorate, then what? Am I even in the
right profession, or just stuck in a rut?
Did I mail off that payment? Did I pick up
my suit? I know I'm forgetting something, is
patience part of the fruit?
We have rehearsal tonight, but I have other
plans. Help the needy and (mostly) greedy?

Lord, I've only got two hands.
There's Bible Study on Wednesdays and
meetings on Mondays. I am practically at
Church from Sunday to Sunday.
You've burned my insides like a craftsman
with gold. Flames set hot and long enough,
gave newness to the old.
My old friends are gone and some family
members too. You've got my attention,
now what must I do?
Dedicate my whole being to focus on You?
Put aside my plans and desires and give
what is due? Should I think of You each
second and meditate each day?
Should I fast and pray and watch what I
say? Should I be humble and obedient and
forget about myself? Shall I, Your vessel,
just sit here on a shelf?
Waiting to be used by You, is that my only
goal? Have you the rights to my spirit and
the papers to my soul?
Pray harder, listen better, study more, and
sin less? And my God silenced me, as I felt
Him say..."Yes!"

"Whatever I command, you should do with
no delay. You must study My Words and
walk in My Way.
I will cleanse you, from all you have done
to yourself. For you know not the time,
you'll be pulled from the shelf.
Like a glass that is dirty, with smudges and
spots, you must be presentable, having no
blots.
For My Living Water must be sweet to
the taste. Therefore, I must prepare the
container in which it is placed.
Your life is not yours, it belongs to Me. I
knew you before you knew, now I want you
to see.
Your true purpose in life is based on My
plans. So, I will mold you and shape you
with My own hands.
Yes, pain you feel and experience loss. But
it's not as though I asked you to carry a
Cross.
Who has stretched you wide and speared
you deep? Who has nailed your hands and
pierced your feet?

Are there stripes on your back, or bruises
on your face? When was the last time you
saved the human race?
Have you died lately and arisen from the
dead? Did I ask you to adorn a crown of
thorns upon your head?
My Son wore that crown so that yours may
be one of glory, now all I'm asking of you, is
to tell the story.
Tell them where you were when you heard
the Good News. How you came to know
that Jesus paid all your dues.
So, yes, you owe Me. But your life is not the
fine. As a matter of fact, you're only giving
Me back what's already Mine.
Just do what you must and give it your
best. Don't worry, just have faith and I'll
take care of the rest.
I love you and want you to trust and
choose Me. You must My dear child, if you
want to be free.
Free from the powers and bondage of sin.
Able to choose eternal life instead of an
eternal end.

I want Us to be close on one accord."
Then His eyes asked if I understood and I
humbly replied... "Yes, Lord."
- Anonymous

I don't know who wrote this poem, but I have been carrying it for many years just to share with you. I cry, I cry, and I cry when I read it because with all of our stuff going on and as we complain, God is right; HE did not ask us to carry that cross. Envision and remember even how hard it was for Jesus to do it. It reminds us that even Jesus had a plan and purpose and He finished his course. Now, what is wrong with us? What do we have to complain about? What do we have to be fearful of? What is keeping us from walking in our ministry, pursuing our desires? Walking in love and forgiveness? Encouraging others? Walking in our purpose?

So, get moving with life. Trust God! God bless you! I love you! So excited for you!

"Commit thy way unto the LORD; Trust also
in him; And he shall bring it to pass."
- Psalm 37:5-6

God has shown me that He truly desires to have a relationship with us, a trust relationship. I recently heard Him say to me, "Trust ME, if you are going to trust anything or anyone, surely trust ME and My promises!" Wow!

In reflecting, the only thing I can remember my mother ever telling me about God was that HE was a faithful God, as she was nearing transition. She said, "God is a faithful God," with tears in her eyes and so much conviction on her face. I find myself often repeating her saying that, in my head. Another treasure in my treasure box.

There will be many things in this world that try to persuade you to trust anything other than God, be careful who you trust on this glorious faith-walk. God promises to give us what we need to flourish.

Are you holding on to things God wants you to let go of that may keep you from trusting Him?

Once upon a time, there was a cheerful little girl with bouncy curls who was almost five. Waiting with her mother at the checkout stand, she saw them, a circle of glistening white pearls in a pink foil box. "Oh, Mommy. Please, Mommy, can I have them? Please, Mommy, please?"

Quickly, the mother checked the back of the little foil box and then looked back at the pleading pretty eyes of her little girl's upturned face. "At $1.95, that is almost $2.00. If you really want them, I will think of some extra chores for you and in no time, you can save enough money to buy them for yourself. Your birthday's only a week away and you might get another crispy dollar bill from Grandma."

As soon as Jenny got home, she emptied her penny bank and counted out seventeen pennies. After dinner, she did more than her share of chores, and she went to the neighbor and asked Mrs. McJames if she could pick dandelions for ten cents. On her birthday, Grandma did give her another new dollar bill. At last, she had enough money to buy the necklace.

Jenny loved her pearls. They made her feel so dressed up and grown up. She wore them everywhere: Sunday school, kindergarten, even to bed. The only time she took them off was when she went swimming or had a bubble bath. Mother said if they got wet, they might turn her neck green.

Jenny had a very loving daddy and every night when she was ready for bed, he would stop whatever he was doing and come upstairs to read her a story. One night, as he finished the story, he asked Jenny, "Do you love me?"

"Oh yes, Daddy. You know that I love you."

"Then give me your pearls."

"Oh Daddy, not the pearls. But you can have Princess, the white horse from my collection, the one with the pink tail. Remember, Daddy? The one you gave me. She is my very favorite."

"That is okay, honey. Daddy loves you. Good night." And he brushed her cheek with a kiss.

About a week later, after the story time, Jenny's daddy asked again, "Do you love me?"

"Daddy, you know I love you."

"Then give me your pearls."

"Oh Daddy, not my pearls. But you can have my baby doll. The brand new one I got for my birthday. She is beautiful and you can have the yellow blanket that matches her sleeper."

"That is okay, sleep well. God bless you, little one. Daddy loves you." And as always, he brushed her cheek with a gentle kiss. A few nights later when her daddy came in, Jenny was sitting on her bed with her legs crossed Indian style. As he came close, he noticed her chin was trembling and one silent tear rolled down her cheek. "What is it, Jenny? What is the matter?" Jenny didn't say anything but lifted her little hand up to her daddy. And when she opened it, there was her little pearl necklace. With a little quiver, she finally said, "Here, Daddy, this is for you."

With tears gathering in his own eyes, Jenny's daddy reached out with one hand to take the dime-store necklace, and with the other hand he reached into his pocket

and pulled out a blue velvet case with a
strand of genuine pearls and gave them
to Jenny. He had them all the time. He was
just waiting for her to give up the dime-
store stuff so he could give her the genuine
treasure.

- Anonymous

So it is with our Heavenly Father. He is waiting for us to give up the cheap things in our lives so that He can give us beautiful treasures. Isn't God good? Are you holding on to things that God wants you to let go of? Are you holding on to harmful or unnecessary patterns, relationships, habits, and activities that you have become so attached to that it seems impossible to let go? Sometimes it is so hard to see what is in the other hand but do believe this one thing: God will never take away something without giving you something better in its place.

God told me, "I am more real than what you see in front of you!" WOW, that was mind blowing – I tucked that deep into my treasure! So, my dear friend, dust yourself off, pull up your bootstraps and commit your life to God and trust with all your heart His promises for your life. This is a faith-walk. And you know the definition of FAITH, right? BELIEVING in what you do not see regardless of what you see today. Are you interested? Let's keep walking!

4

YOUR ARMOR TO STAND. WHEN YOU'VE DONE ALL THAT YOU CAN DO, STAND.

"Above all else, guard your heart for it affects everything you do."
Proverbs 4:23

"Take delight in the Lord and He will give you the desires of your heart." Psalms 37:4

"For I know the plans I have for you, says the Lord, plans for welfare (health-happiness-fortunes) and not for evil, to give you a future and a hope."
Jeremiah 29:11

"I have given you authority to trample on snakes and scorpions and to overcome all the power of the enemy; nothing will harm you."
Luke 10:19

"If one moves confidently in the direction of their dreams, and endeavors to live the life which he has imagined, he will meet with a success unexpected in common hours."
Henry David Thoreau

The armor of God represents the defense we must take in our spiritual lives to be victorious! God wanted me to give this to you. You will need this in your faith-walk – your spiritual warfare. Oh, you thought the enemy was just going to let you move to something better without opposition? Oh, no, no-no.

Pray daily: "I put on the whole armor of God to fight the good fight of faith! I have on the <u>belt of truth</u> and the <u>breastplate of righteousness</u>. My <u>feet are shod in peace (wearing shoes of peace)</u>. I have on the <u>shield of faith</u> to extinguish all the fiery darts of the enemy; no harm shall come to me. I put on the <u>helmet of salvation</u> and battle with the <u>sword of the Spirit</u>, which is the Word of God; I will not be moved!"

How to use the Armor of God in your daily guidance:

The Belt of Truth – "Does this sound right to me?" Pause and ask God about it.

The Breastplate of Righteousness – When trials and temptations come our way.

The Shield of Faith – Doubt and fear are attacks

from the enemy. Read your Scriptures (your sword) to protect you and allow you to fight back against these attacks. "But God's Word says..."

The Shoes of the Gospel of Peace – The feeling of contentment, completeness, wholeness, well-being, harmony, and rest. Peace is God's victory over evil.

The Helmet of Salvation – The helmet protects our mind.

> "Do not conform to the pattern of
> this world but be transformed by
> the renewing of your mind."
> **- Romans 12:2**

The Sword of the Spirit (the Word of God) –

> "For the Word of God is alive and
> active. Sharper than any double-
> edged sword..."
> **- Hebrews 4:12**

Now you are ready to start your days - you are going to battle - go get what God says is already yours!

- Warfare -

"[11] Put on the whole armor of God, so that you will be able to stand firm against all strategies of the devil. [12] For we are not fighting against flesh-and-blood enemies, but against evil rulers and authorities of the unseen world, against mighty powers in this dark world, and against evil spirits in the heavenly places. [13] Wherefore take unto you the whole armor of God, that ye may be able to withstand in the evil day, and having done all, to stand. [14] Stand therefore, having fastened on the belt of truth, and having put on the breastplate of righteousness. [15] For shoes, put on the peace that comes from the Good News so that you will be fully prepared. [16] Above all, take up the shield of faith, with which you can extinguish all the flaming arrows of the evil one. [17] Put on salvation as your helmet, and take the sword of the Spirit, which is the word of God.

[18] And pray in the Spirit on all occasions with all kinds of prayers and requests. With

this in mind, be alert and always keep on praying for all the Lord's people."

- Ephesians 6:11-18:

SCRIPTURES TO STOMP ON FEAR – FALSE EVIDENCE APPEARING REAL

Isaiah 41:10: "Fear not, for I am with you; be not dismayed, for I am your God; I will strengthen you, I will help you, I will uphold you with my righteous right hand."

Deuteronomy 31:8: "The Lord himself goes before you and will be with you; He will never leave you nor forsake you. Do not be afraid; do not be discouraged."

2 Timothy 1:7: "For God did not give us a spirt of fear but a SPIRIT of POWER, of LOVE and of Self Discipline."

Psalm 27:1: "The Lord is my light and my salvation; whom shall I fear? The Lord is the stronghold of my life; of whom shall I be afraid?"

Psalm 56:3–4: "When I am afraid, I put my trust in You. In God, whose word I praise—in God I trust. I will not be afraid. What can man do to me?"

Psalm 34:4–5: "I sought the Lord, and he answered me and delivered me from all my fears. Those who look to him are radiant, and their faces shall never be ashamed."

Deuteronomy 31:6: "Be strong and courageous. Do not be afraid or terrified because of them, for the LORD your God goes with you; He will never leave you nor forsake you."

SCRIPTURES TO TRUST IN GOD

Proverbs 3:5-6: "Trust in the Lord with all your heart, and do not lean on your own understanding. In all your ways acknowledge Him, and He will make straight your paths."

Psalm 37:3-5: "Trust in the Lord and do good; dwell in the land and befriend faithfulness. Delight yourself in the Lord and He will give you the desires of your heart. Commit your way to the Lord; trust in Him, and He will act."

Psalm 143:8: "Let me hear in the morning of your steadfast love for in You I trust. Make me know the way I should go, for to You I lift up my soul."

Proverbs 16:3: "Commit your work to the Lord and your plans will be established."

Jeremiah 29:11: "For I know the plans I have for you, declares the Lord, plans for welfare and not for evil, to give you a future and a hope."

Philippians 4:13: "I can do all things through Christ, who strengthens me."

Philippians 4:6-7: "Do not be anxious about anything, but in every situation, by prayer and petition, with thanksgiving, present your requests to God. And the peace of God, which transcends all understanding, will guard your hearts and your minds in Christ Jesus."

Luke 10:19: "I have given you authority to trample on snakes and scorpions and to overcome all the power of the enemy; nothing will harm you."

SCRIPTURES OF FAITH

Hebrews 11:1: "Now faith is the assurance of things hoped for, the conviction/evidence of things not seen."

Hebrews 11:16: "Without faith, it is impossible to please God, because anyone who comes to him must believe that He exists and that He rewards those who earnestly seek Him."

Mark 9:23: "Jesus said to him, 'If you can believe? All things are possible for one who believes.'"

Matthew 15:28: "Then Jesus answered her, 'O woman, great is your faith! Be it done for you as you desire.' And her daughter was healed instantly."

Matthew 17:20: "Truly I tell you, if you have faith as small as a mustard seed, you can say to this mountain, 'Move from here to there,' and it will move. Nothing will be impossible for you."

Matthew 21:22: "And whatever you ask in prayer, you will receive, if you have faith."

2 Corinthians 5:7: "For we walk by faith, not by sight."

James 1:6: "But when you ask, you must believe and not doubt, because the one who doubts is like a wave of the sea, blown and tossed by the wind."

1 John 5:4: "That's because everyone who is a child of God has won the battle over the world. Our faith has won the battle for us"

1 Timothy 6:11: "But you, man of God, flee from all this, and pursue righteousness, godliness, faith, love, endurance and gentleness."

Hebrews 11:11: "And by faith even Sarah, who

was past childbearing age, was enabled to bear children because she considered him faithful who had made the promise."

Romans 1:17: "For in the gospel the righteousness of God is revealed—a righteousness that is by faith from first to last, just as it is written: 'The righteous will live by faith.'"

Romans 10:11: "As Scripture says, 'Anyone who believes in Him will never be put to shame.'"

BE YOU. BE LOVE. BE FREE.

"Above all else, guard your heart for it affects everything
you do."
Proverbs 4:23

"Take delight in the Lord and He will give you the desires of
your heart." Psalms 37:4

"For I know the plans I have for you, says the Lord, plans
for welfare (health-happiness-fortunes) and not for evil, to
give you a future and a hope."
Jeremiah 29:11

"I have given you authority to trample on snakes and
scorpions and to overcome all the power of the enemy;
nothing will harm you."
Luke 10:19

"If one moves confidently in the direction of their dreams,
and endeavors to live the life which he has imagined, he
will meet with a success unexpected in common hours."
Henry David Thoreau

An abundant and beautiful life is our birthright. Let's give ourselves permission to create what's already ours! Life isn't about finding yourself — life is about CREATING yourself. Who knew?

Let's move through life in unquestioning FAITH, FREEDOM, LOVE, PEACE, ABUNDANCE, POWER, EXCITEMENT, and INTRIGUE while realizing everything you could want exists within you. You create your life from within. God lives within. We co-create with God. Let's get busy co-creating with God from within.

Finally, brothers and sisters,
whatever is true, whatever is noble,
whatever is right, whatever is pure,
whatever is lovely, whatever is
admirable — if anything is excellent
or praiseworthy — think about such
things.
- Philippians 4:8

NOTES/PRAYERS

NOTES/PRAYERS

NOTES/PRAYERS

NOTES/PRAYERS

NOTES/PRAYERS

NOTES/PRAYERS

ABOUT THE AUTHOR

Nakita is a business owner. She has her own executive search firm and she is a career coach. She uses her ministry, To Encourage People to Dream and To Have Hope and To Know That with God, ALL Things Are Possible, to minister to the homeless through her church, at transitional living facilities, and to all she sees along the way. She is a mom to three very loved kitty cats — Gracie, Oliver, Miley — who enjoy prayer time as well.

Monthly web-conferences will be held for Book Expressions and to help you where you may need it. Please email me at: Yes@EvenMeGod.com for more information and the class schedule. I would encourage you to keep a journal of your journey because I can assure you, it is going to be an exciting one for you with God.

NOTES/QUESTIONS FOR YOUR
MONTHLY WEBINARS WITH THE AUTHOR.

NOTES/QUESTİONS FOR YOUR
MONTHLY WEBİNARS WİTH THE AUTHOR.

NOTES/QUESTIONS FOR YOUR MONTHLY WEBINARS WITH THE AUTHOR.

NOTES/QUESTIONS FOR YOUR MONTHLY WEBINARS WITH THE AUTHOR.

NOTES/QUESTIONS FOR YOUR
MONTHLY WEBINARS WITH THE AUTHOR.

NOTES/QUESTIONS FOR YOUR
MONTHLY WEBINARS WITH THE AUTHOR.

www.ingramcontent.com/pod-product-compliance
Lightning Source LLC
Chambersburg PA
CBHW060910130726
48001CB00006B/2175